Celebrate, Remember
Celebrar, Recordar

Bilingual Music for Weddings and Funerals
Music Bilingüe para Bodas y Funerales

by
The Collegeville Composers Group

LITURGICAL PRESS
Collegeville, Minnesota

www.litpress.org

Celebrate, Remember is a bilingual resource for Weddings and Funerals. All the music can be sung in either English or Spanish or with both languages in alternation. The music can be sung *a cappella* with just cantor and assembly, but accompaniments are provided for keyboard, guitar, and also choir descants and harmonies.

Celebrar, Recordar es un recurso bilingüe para Bodas y Funerales. Toda la música puede ser cantada en Inglés o Español o alternando ambos idiomas. La música puede ser cantada a capella con sólo un cantor y asamblea, pero acompañamientos se proporcionan para teclado, guitarra, y también para coro con contrapuntos y armonías.

ADDITIONAL RESOURCES

A CD recording is also available: 978-0-8146-7977-7.

ACKNOWLEDGEMENTS

Cover design by Ann Blattner. Cover photo: Thinkstock.

ISBN 978-0-8146-4811-7

Contents

Fill Us with Your Love, O Lord / *Sácianos con Tu Amor*

Wedding Entrance Processional / *Entrada Procesional para Bodas*

peace. Fill us with your love, O Lord, as we
tan. Sá - cia - nos con tu a - mor; da - nos
peace, fill us, Lord, as we
paz, da - nos luz, da - nos
peace, give us peace. Fill us, fill us with your love, O
paz, da nos paz. Sá - cia - nos, sá - cia - nos con tu a -
(G sus4) B♭sus4 (G) B♭ (C) E♭ (F/C) A♭/E♭ (Cmaj7) E♭maj7 (C6) E♭6
place our lives in your hands.
luz, da - nos go - zo y paz.
place our lives in your hands.
luz, da - nos go - zo y paz.
Lord, O Lord.
mor, Se - ñor.
(F) A♭ (C) E♭

Verses / Estrofas Ps 37(36): 3-4a, 5-6a, 7, 18-19a, 21-22a, 23a+24, 27-28, 39-40a

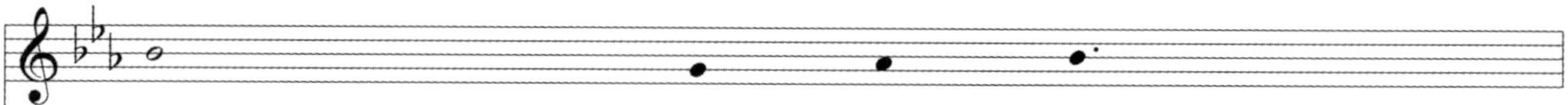

1. If you trust in the Lord	and	do		good,
2. Commit your life	to	the		Lord,
3. Be still be -	fore	the		Lord
4. God protects the lives	of	the		upright,
5. The wicked borrow with -	out	re	-	paying,
6. The Lord guards the steps	of	the		upright
7. Then turn away from evil	and	do		good
8. The salvation of the just comes	from	the		Lord,
1. Confía en el Señor y	*haz*	*el*		*bien,*
2. Encomienda al Señor	*tus*	*em*	-	*presas,*
3. Cállate ante	*el*	*Se*	-	*ñor*
4. El Señor cuida los dias	*de*	*los*		*buenos,*
5. El impió pide fiado y	*no*	*de*	-	*vuelve,*
6. El Señor guia los pa -	*sos*	*del*		*hombre;*
7. Apártate del mal y	*haz*	*el*		*bien,*
8. La salvación de los justos viene	*del*	*Se*	-	*ñor,*

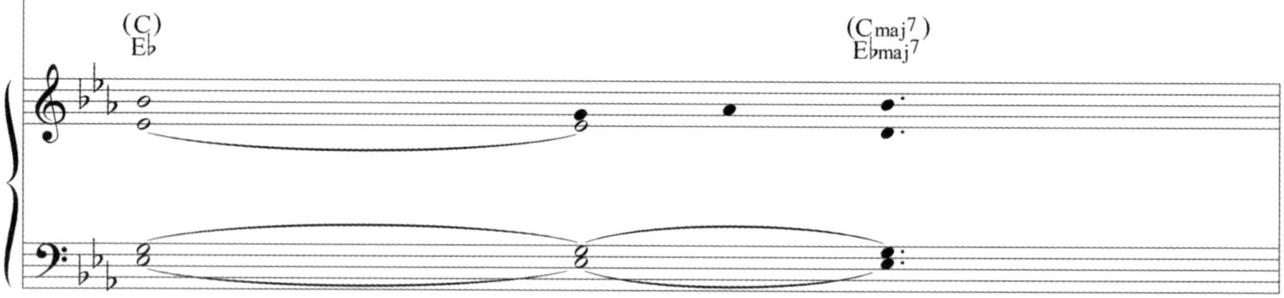

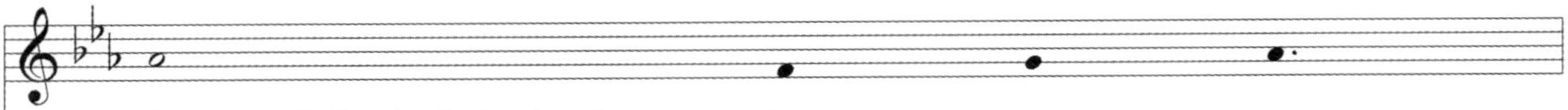

1. then you will live in the land and be se - cure.
2. be confident, and God will act,
3. and wait in patience;
4. their heritage will last for ever.
5. but the just are gene - rous and give.
6. though they stumble they shall ne - ver fall
7. and you shall have a home for ever;
8. their stronghold in time of dis - tress.

1. habita en tu tierra y co - me tran - quilo.
2. confía en él que lo‿ha - rá bien.
3. [–] y es - péralo;
4. su herencia se - rá e - terna.
5. pero el justo es compasivo y com - parte.
6. si el bueno cae, no se que - da en tierra,
7. y tendrás una casa pa - ra siempre.
8. él es su refugio en tiempos de an - gustia.

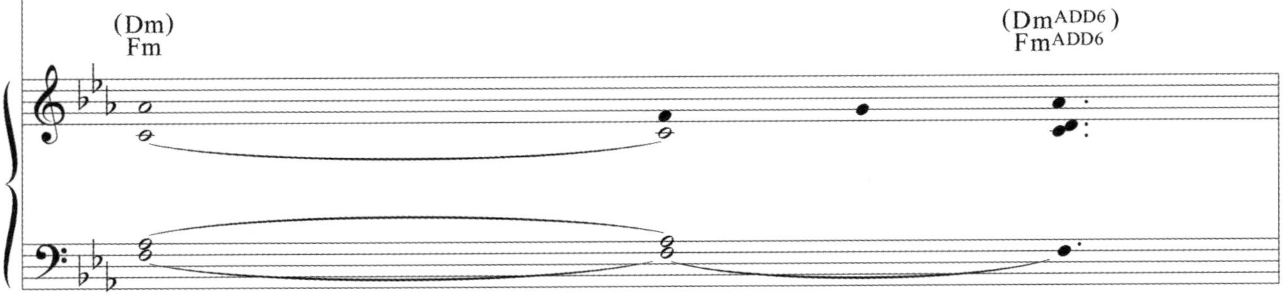

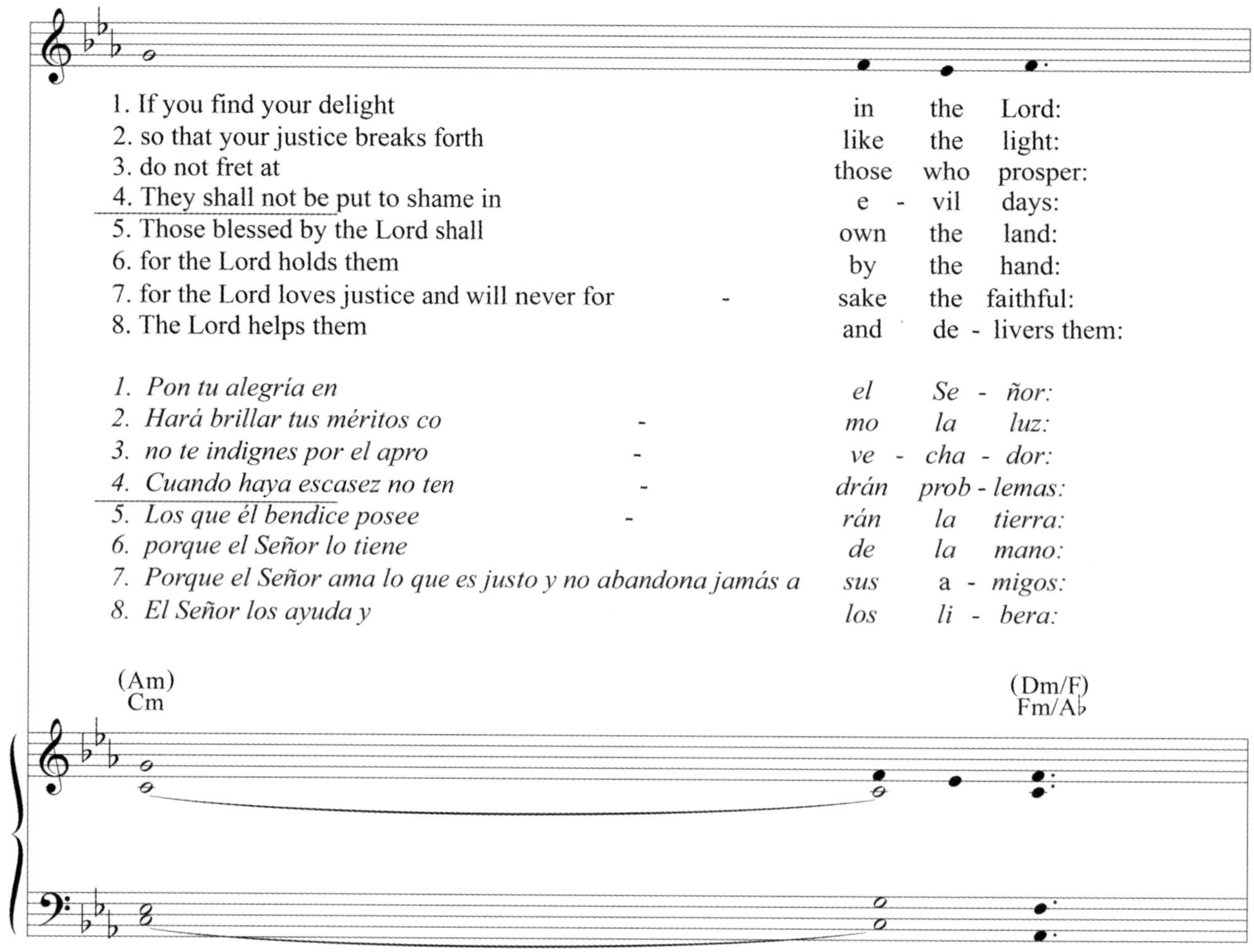
1. If you find your delight in the Lord:
2. so that your justice breaks forth like the light:
3. do not fret at those who prosper:
4. They shall not be put to shame in e - vil days:
5. Those blessed by the Lord shall own the land:
6. for the Lord holds them by the hand:
7. for the Lord loves justice and will never for - sake the faithful:
8. The Lord helps them and de - livers them:
1. Pon tu alegría en el Se - ñor:
2. Hará brillar tus méritos co - mo la luz:
3. no te indignes por el apro - ve - cha - dor:
4. Cuando haya escasez no ten - drán prob - lemas:
5. Los que él bendice posee - rán la tierra:
6. porque el Señor lo tiene de la mano:
7. Porque el Señor ama lo que es justo y no abandona jamás a sus a - migos:
8. El Señor los ayuda y los li - bera:
(Am)
Cm
(Dm/F)
Fm/A♭

All / Todos
1-8. Fill us with your love, O Lord.
1-8. Sá - cia - nos con tu a - mor.
(F)
A♭
(C)
E♭

Dichosos Los que Aman de Todo Corazón / How Happy Are Those who Love with All Their Heart

Wedding Responsorial Psalm / *Salmo Responsorial para Bodas*

♩ = ca. 116

Antiphon / Antífona *Sing twice each time, once in Spanish and then immediately once in English*
Cantar dos veces cada vez, una vez en español y luego inmediatamente una vez en Inglés

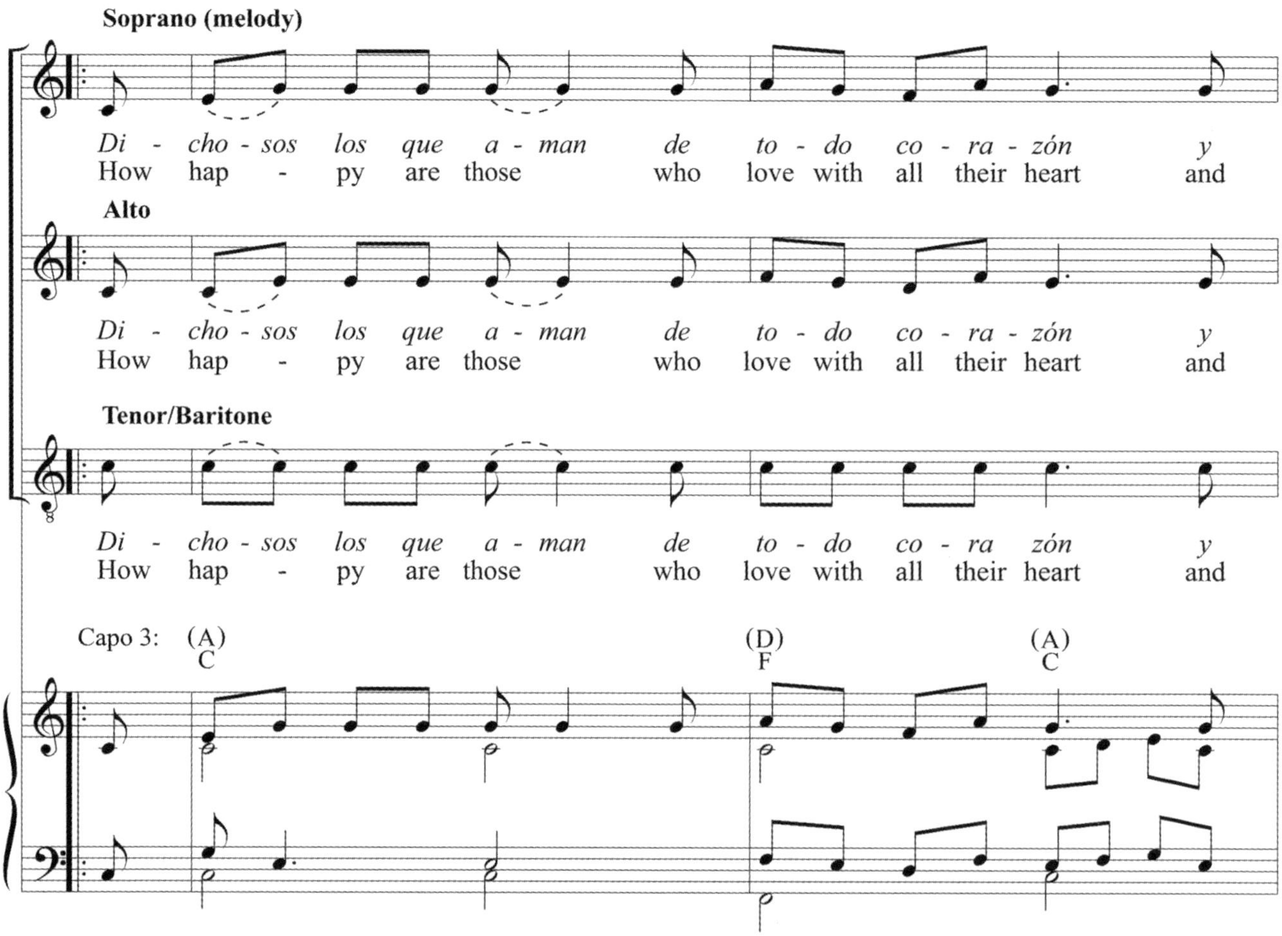

Every time except Final
Cada vez menos Final
Final
si - guen los ca - mi - nos del Se - nor. ñor.
fol - low in the ways of the Lord. Lord.
si guen los ca mi nos del Se ñor. ñor.
fol - low in the ways of the Lord. Lord.
si - guen los ca - mi - nos del Se - ñor. ñor.
fol - low in the ways of the Lord. Lord.
(G) B♭
(D6/F♯) F6/A
(ESUS4) GSUS4
(E) G
(A) C

Verses / Estrofas cf. Ps 112(111): 1, 2, 3, 4, 5, 6, 7-8, 9

Sing each pair of verses before returning to the Antiphon
Cantar cada par de estrofas antes de regresar a la antifona

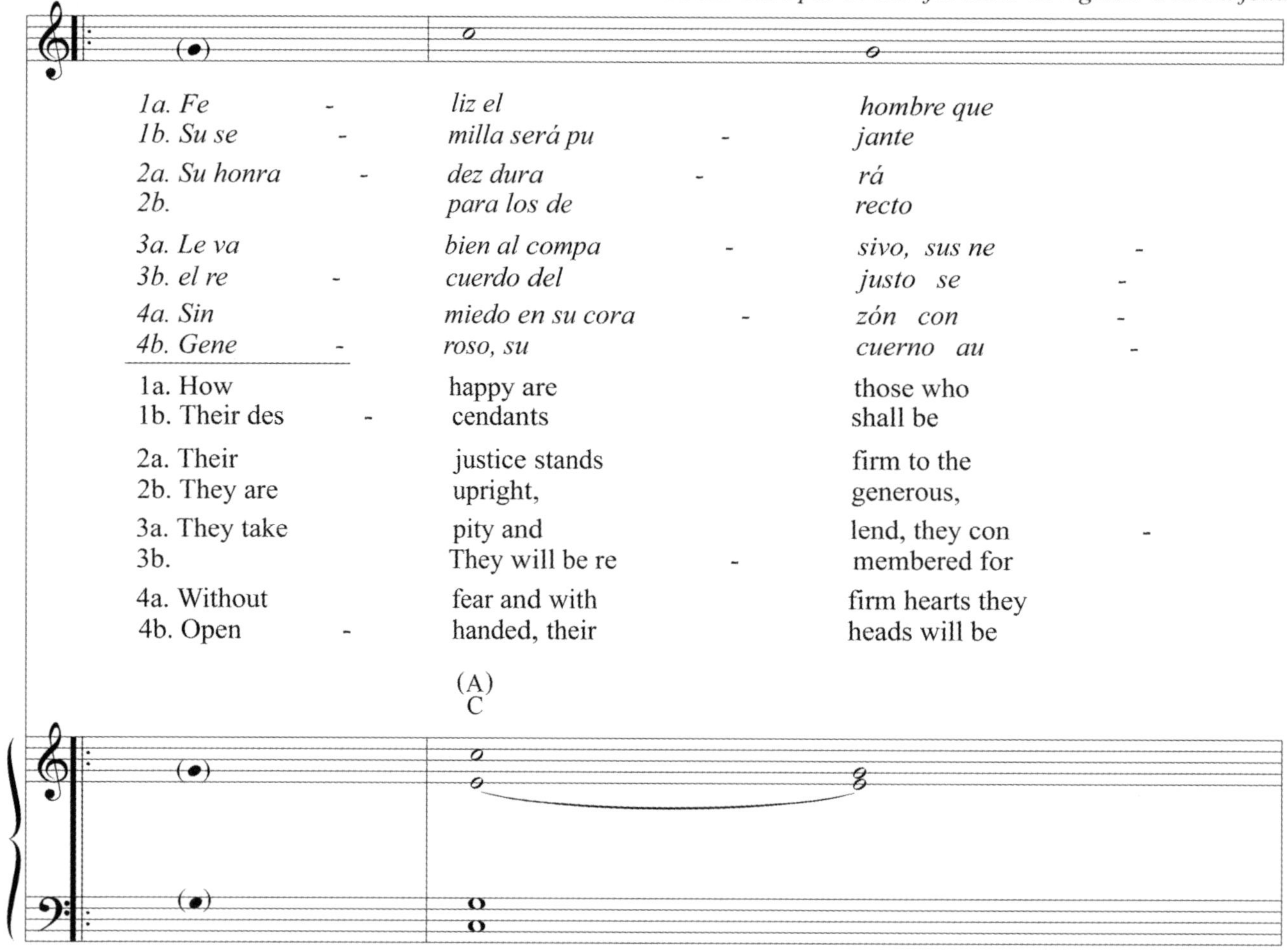

Sing in the language that the cantor has just used in the verse
Cantar en el idioma que el cantor utiliza en la estrofa
1a. teme al Se - ñor: y si - guen los ca - mi - nos del Se - ñor.
1b. en el pa - is: they fol - low in the ways of the Lord.
2a. pa - ra siempre:
2b. co ra - zón:
3a. gocios en con - ciencia.
3b. rá e - terno:
4a. fia en el Se - ñor:
4b. men - ta en gloria:
1a. love with all their heart:
1b. rulers of the earth:
2a. ends of the earth:
2b. merci - ful and just:
3a. duct them - selves with honor:
3b. e - ver - more:
4a. trust in the Lord:
4b. raised in glory:
Sing in the language that the cantor has just used in the verse
Cantar en el idioma que el cantor utiliza en la estrofa
y si - guen los ca - mi - nos del Se - ñor.
they fol - low in the ways of the Lord.
Sing in the language that the cantor has just used in the verse
Cantar en el idioma que el cantor utiliza en la estrofa
y si - guen los ca - mi - nos del Se - ñor.
they fol - low in the ways of the Lord.
(D) F
(A) C
(G) B♭
(D6/F♯) F6/A
(ESUS4) GSUS4
(E) G

Thanks be to God / *Gracias a Dios*

(Acclamation after Exchange of Vows/Exchange of Rings) /
(Aclamación después de Intercambio de Votos/Intercambio de Anillos)

Melody: *Adoro te devote* (Gregorian Chant)
Published and administered by the Liturgical Press, Collegeville, MN 56321.

(Em7) F♯m7 (Am) Bm (Dm7) Em7 (C/E) D/F♯ (F) G (Am7) Bm7 (Dm) Em
1. For the fu - ture life they'll share, thanks be to God!
2. For the Word that makes us one,
3. For com - mit - ment ma - ni - fest,
4. For the joy we ce - le - brate,
5. For the sound of fes - tal song,
1. Por lo que com - par - ti - rán, ¡gra - cias a Dios!
2. Por la ge - ne - ro - si - dad,
3. Por mu - tua fi - de - li - dad,
4. Por el go - zo al ce - le - brar,
5. Que se a - men hoy, Se - ñor,
(ah)
thanks be to God! or
¡gra - cias a Dios!
(Am) Bm (C/G) D/A (F) G F(maj7/C) Gmaj7/D (C) D
1. For their trust and self - less care, thanks be to God!
2. lov - ing pre - sence of the Son,
3. For a life - time al - ways blest,
4. For these lives we con - se - crate,
5. e - v'ry - thing for which we long,
1. y el cui - da - do que ten - drán, ¡gra - cias a Dios!
2. y el a - mor que es ser - vi - cial,
3. Por con - fian - za y su an - he - lar,
4. Por es - te a - le - gre can - tar,
5. co - mo Cris - to nos a - mo,
(ah)
thanks be to God! or
¡gra - cias a Dios!

Live On in My Love

(Verses) All:
Antiphon / Melody
live on in my love. Live on in my love, live on in my love.
Alto Descant
Live on in my love. Live on in my love, live on in my love.
Tenor Descant
Live on in my love. Live on in my love, live on in my love.
Bass Descant
Live on in my love, live on in my love.
D/F♯ G A D Em/G Bm Em7 Em7/G Bm

Vivan en Mi Amor

Estrofas *Juan 15:9, 10, 13, 15, 16; 14:27; Mateo 28:20*

(Estrofas) Todos:
Antífona / Melodia
vi - van en mi a-mor. Vi - van en mi a-mor, vi - van en mi a-mor.
Contrapunto Alto
vi - van en mi a-mor. Vi - van en mi a-mor, vi - van en mi a-mor.
Contrapunto Tenor
vi - van en mi a-mor. Vi - van en mi a-mor, vi - van en mi a-mor.
Contrapunto Bajo
Vi - van en mi a-mor, vi - van en mi a-mor.
D/F♯ G A D Em/G Bm Em7 Em7/G Bm

Love Bears All Things

Verse Tone

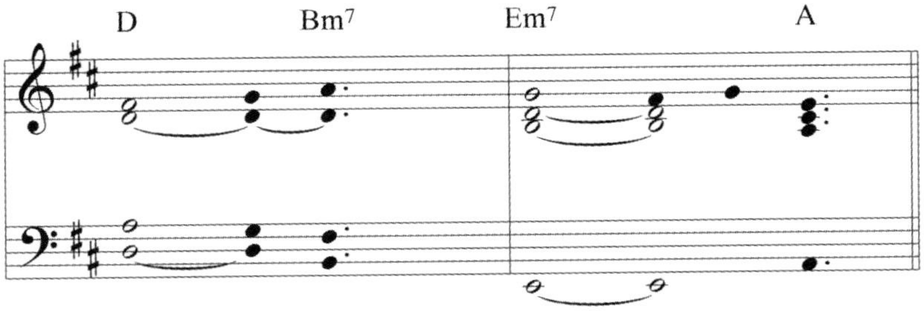

John 15:16-17; 1 Corinthians 13:4-5a, 6, 13, 8a; 14:1a

1. You did not choose me
   but I chose you.

2. And I appointed you to go and bear fruit,
   fruit that will last,

3. so that the Father will give you
   whatever you ask him in my name.

4. I am giving you these commands
   so that you may love one another.

5. Love is patient; love is kind;
   love is not envious or boastful or arrogant or rude.

6. Love does not rejoice in wrongdoing,
   but rejoices in the truth.

7. Faith, hope and love abide, these three;
   and the greatest of these is love.

8. Love never ends.
   Pursue love and strive for the spiritual gifts.

El Amor Soporta Todo

Tono des Estrofas

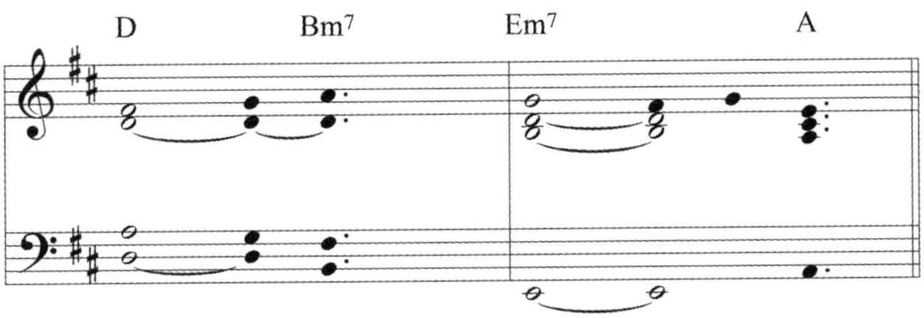

Juan 15:16-17; 1 Corintios 13:4-5a, 6, 13, 8a; 14:1a

1. Ustedes no me eligieron a mí;
   he sido yo quien los eligió a ustedes

2. y los preparé para que vayan y den fruto,
   y ese fruto permanezca.

3. Así es como el Padre les concederá
   todo lo que le pidan en mi Nombre.

4. Amense los unos a los otros:
   esto es lo que les mando.

5. El amor es paciente y muestra comprensión.
   El amor no tiene celos, no aparenta ni se infla,
   no actúa con bajeza.

6. No se alegra de lo_injusto,
   sino que se goza en la verdad.

7. Ahora, pues, son válidas la fe, la esperanza y el amor:
   las tres;
   pero la mayor de estas tres es el amor.

8. El amor nunca pasará.
   Busquen el amor y aspiren a los dones espirituales.

Merciful and Tender, Faithful Is the Lord

Antiphon ♩ = ca. 100

Verse Tone

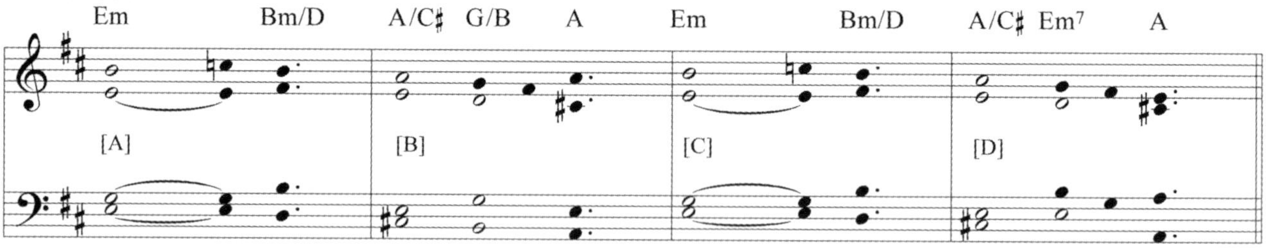

Psalm 103: 1-2, 3-4, 8. 10, 11-12, 17-18, 19-20, 21-22

1. My soul, give thanks to the LORD,
   all my being, bless God's holy name.
   My soul, give thanks to the LORD
   and never forget all God's blessings.

2. It is God who forgives all your guilt,
   who heals every one of your ills,
   who redeems your life from the grave,
   who crowns you with love and compassion,
   [repeat C-D]
   who fills your life with good things,
   renewing your youth like an eagle's.

3. The LORD is compassion and love,
   slow to anger and rich in mercy.
   God does not treat us according to our sins
   nor repay us according to our faults.

4. For as the heavens are high above the earth
   so strong is God's love for the God-fearing;
   as far as the east is from the west
   so far does he remove our sins.

5. *A* But the love of the LORD is everlasting
   B upon those who fear the LORD.
   A God's justice reaches out to children's children
   B when they keep his covenant in truth,
   D when they keep his will in their mind.

6. *A* The LORD has set his throne in heaven
   B and his kingdom rules over all.
   A Give thanks to the LORD, all you angels,
   B mighty in power, fulfilling God's word,
   D who heed the voice of that word.

7. *A* Give thanks to the LORD, all you hosts,
   B you servants who do God's will.
   A Give thanks to the LORD, all his works,
   B in every place where God rules.
   D My soul, give thanks to the LORD!

Clemente y Bondadoso, Fiel es el Señor

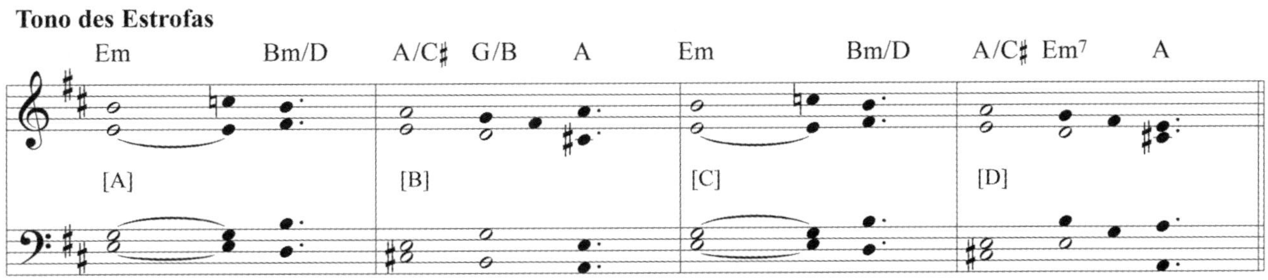

Salmo 103(102): 1-2, 3-4, 8. 10, 11-12, 17-18, 19-20, 21-22

1. Bendice al Señor, alma mía,
 alabe todo mi ser su santo Nombre.
 Bendice, alma mía, al Señor,
 y no olvides ninguno de sus beneficios.

2. El perdona todas tus ofensas
 y te cura de todas tus dolencias.
 El rescata tu vida de la tumba,
 te corona de amor y de ternura.
[repetid C-D]
 El colma de dicha tu existencia
 y como el águila se renueva tu juventud.

3. El Señor es ternura y compasión,
 lento a la cólera y lleno de‿amor;
 No nos trata según nuestros pecados
 ni nos paga según nuestras ofensas.

4. Cuanto se alzan los cielos sobre la tierra
 tan alto es su amor con los que le temen.
 Como el oriente está lejos del occidente
 así aleja de nosotros nuestras culpas.

5. *A* Pero el amor del Señor con los que le temen
 B es desde siempre y para siempre;
 A defenderá a los hijos de sus hijos,
 B de aquellos que guardan su alianza
 D y se acuerdan de cumplir sus ordenanzas.

6. *A* El Señor ha fijado su trono en los cielos
 B y su realeza todo lo domina.
 A Bendigan al Señor todos sus ángeles,
 B héroes poderosos, que ejecutan sus órdenes
 D apenas oyen el sonido de su palabra.

7. *A* Bendigan al Señor todos sus ejércitos,
 B sus servidores, para hacer su voluntad.
 A Bendigan al Señor todas sus obras,
 B en todos los lugares de su dominio.
 D ¡Bendice, alma mía, al Señor!

Dales el Descanso Eterno, Señor / Grant Eternal Rest to Your Servants, O Lord

Funeral Entrance or Communion Chant / Canto de Entrada o Canto de Comunión para Funerales

Verses / Estrofas *Ps 27(26): 1, 4, 5, 7-8, 8c-9c, 9de-10, 13-14*

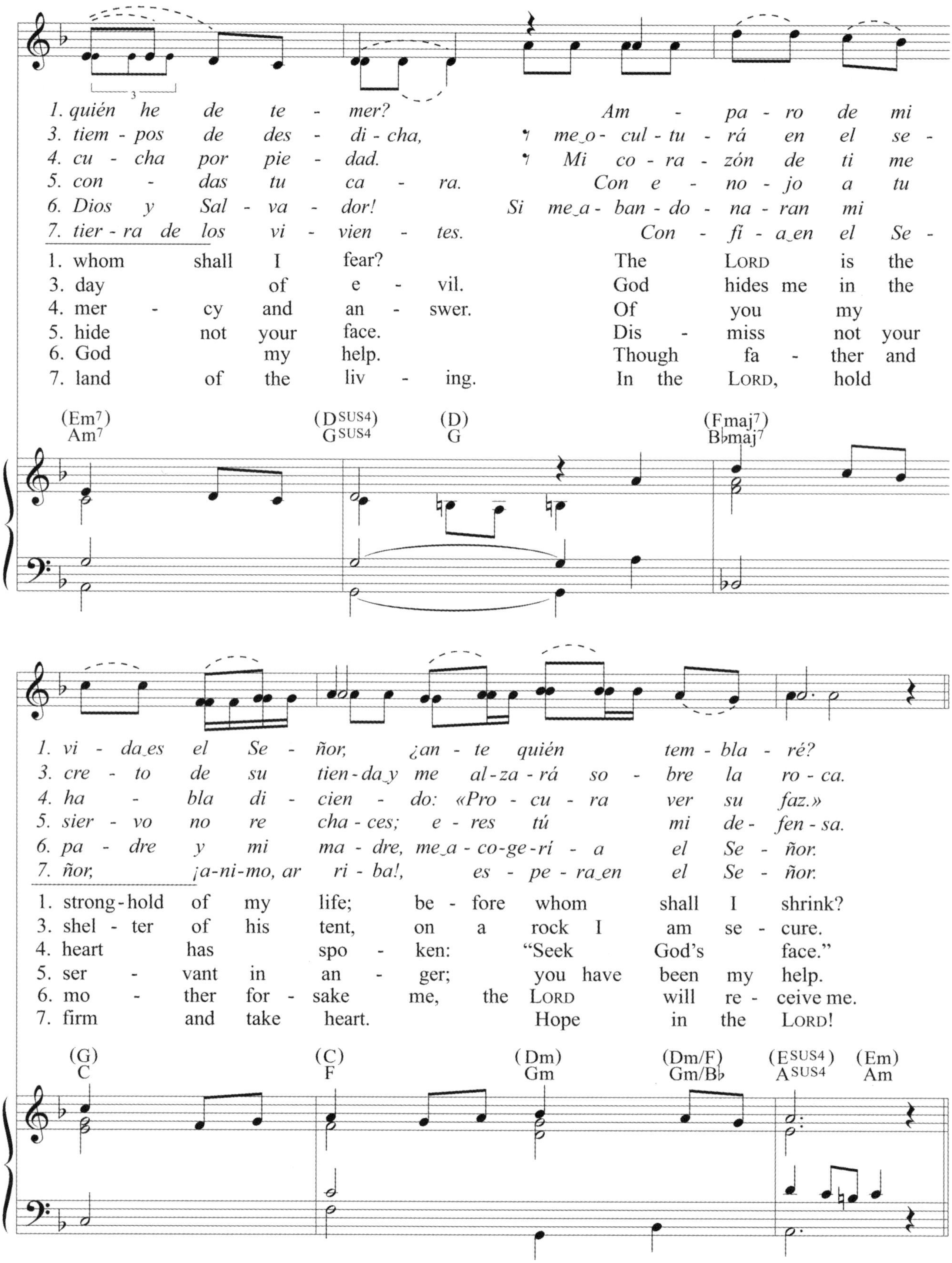
1. quién he de te - mer? Am - pa - ro de mi
3. tiem - pos de des - di - cha, me_o - cul - tu - rá en el se -
4. cu - cha por pie - dad. Mi co - ra - zón de ti me
5. con - das tu ca - ra. Con e - no - jo a tu
6. Dios y Sal - va - dor! Si me_a - ban - do - na - ran mi
7. tier - ra de los vi - vien - tes. Con - fi - a_en el Se -
1. whom shall I fear? The LORD is the
3. day of e - vil. God hides me in the
4. mer - cy and an - swer. Of you my
5. hide not your face. Dis - miss not your
6. God my help. Though fa - ther and
7. land of the liv - ing. In the LORD, hold
(Em7) Am7 (DSUS4) GSUS4 (D) G (Fmaj7) B♭maj7
1. vi - da_es el Se - ñor, ¿an - te quién tem - bla - ré?
3. cre - to de su tien - da_y me al - za - rá so - bre la ro - ca.
4. ha - bla di - cien - do: «Pro - cu - ra ver su faz.»
5. sier - vo no re cha - ces; e - res tú mi de - fen - sa.
6. pa - dre y mi ma - dre, me_a - co - ge - rí - a el Se - ñor.
7. ñor, ¡a-ni-mo, ar ri - ba!, es - pe - ra_en el Se - ñor.
1. strong - hold of my life; be - fore whom shall I shrink?
3. shel - ter of his tent, on a rock I am se - cure.
4. heart has spo - ken: "Seek God's face."
5. ser - vant in an - ger; you have been my help.
6. mo - ther for - sake me, the LORD will re - ceive me.
7. firm and take heart. Hope in the LORD!
(G) C (C) F (Dm) Gm (Dm/F) Gm/B♭ (ESUS4) ASUS4 (Em) Am

Verse / Estrofa 2
2. U - na co - sa al Se - ñor só - lo le pi - do, la co - sa que yo bus - co es ha - bi -
2. There is one thing I ask of the LORD, for this I long, to
(Am) Dm (Em7/F) Am7/C (F) B♭ (Em7) Am7 (DSUS4) (D) GSUS4 G
tar en la ca - sa del Se - ñor mien - tras du - re mi vi - da, pa - ra go -
live in the house of the LORD all the days of my life, to
(Fmaj7) B♭maj7 (G) C (C) F (Dm) Gm (Dm/F) Gm/B♭ (ESUS4) (Em) ASUS4 Am
zar de la dul - zu - ra del Se - ñor y cui - dar de su san - tua - rio.
sa - vor the sweet - ness of the LORD, to be - hold his tem - ple.
(Fmaj7) B♭maj7 (G) C (C) F (Dm) Gm (Dm/F) Gm/B♭ (ESUS4) (Em) ASUS4 Am

From Clay You Have Shaped Me / *De Barro Me Formaste*

Funeral Responsorial Psalm / *Salmo Responsorial para Funerales*

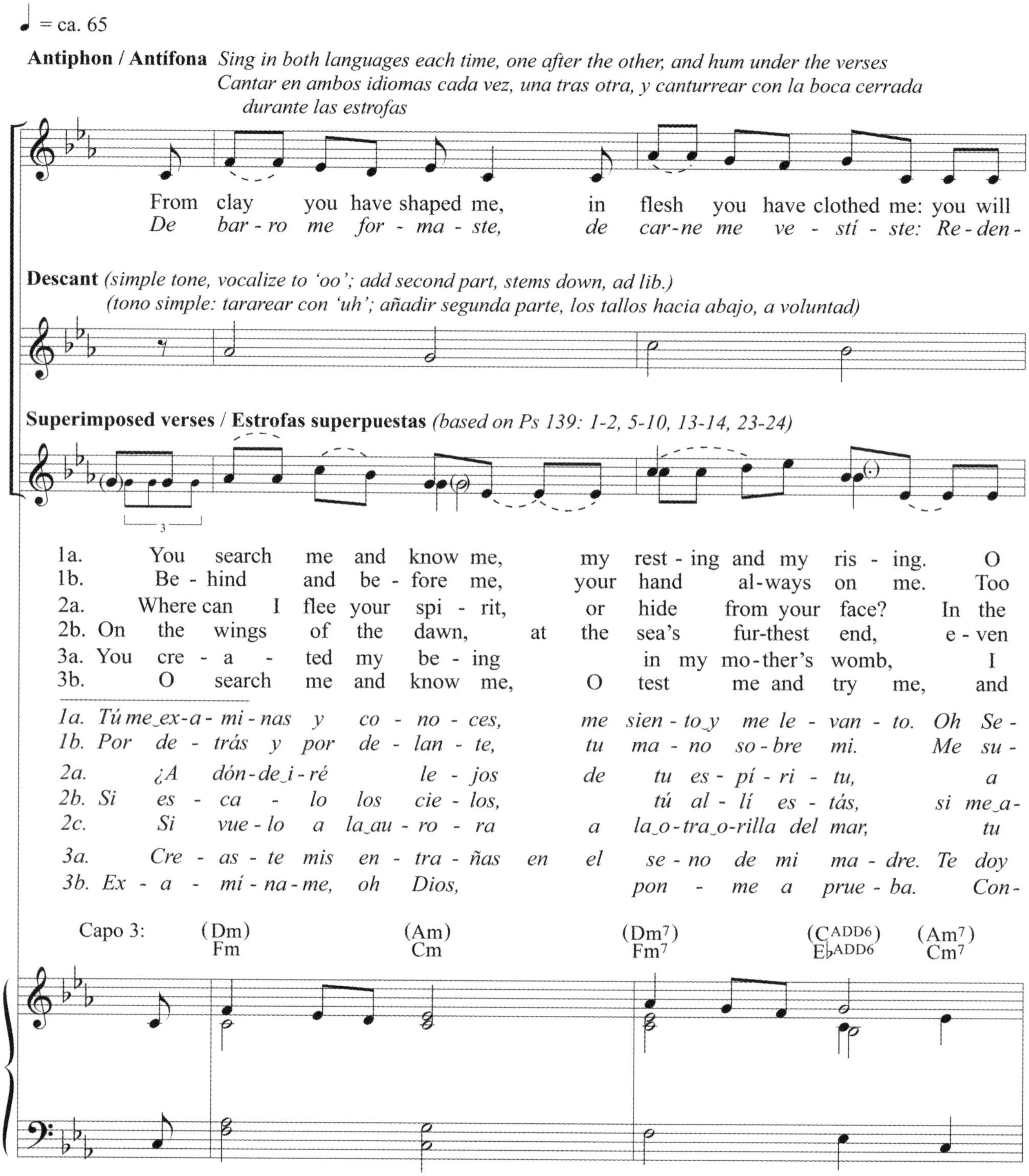

Published and administered by the Liturgical Press, Collegeville, MN 56321.

raise me on the last day, my Re - deem - er and Lord.
tor, re - su - scí - ta - me‿en el dí - a fi - nal.
1a. LORD, all my ways lie o - pen to you.
1b. won - der - ful this know - ledge, too high be - yond my reach.
2a. hea - vens you are there, in the grave you are there.
2b. there your hand would lead me, your right hand hold me fast.
3a. thank you for the won - ders of all your cre - a - tion.
3b. lead me in the path of e - ter - nal life.
1a. ñor, tu‿e - res tes - ti - go de to - dos mi pa - sos.
1b. pe - ra‿e - se pro - di - gio, pro - di - gio de sa - ber.
2a. dón - de hu - i - ré le - jos de tu ro - stro?
2b. cues - to‿en - tre los muer - tos, al - lí tam - bien es - tás.
2c. ma - no me con - du - ce y me tie - ne tu de - re - cha.
3a. gra - cias por tan - tas ma - ra - vil - las en tus o - bras.
3b. dú - ce - me por la sen - da de vi - da e - ter - na.
(F) A♭
(Cmaj7/E) E♭maj7/G
(Dm) Fm
(Dm/F) Fm/A♭
(E) G

Dios Enjugará Cada Una de Sus Lágrimas / God Will Wipe Away Every Tear from Their Eyes

Funeral Communion Psalm / *Salmo de Comunión para Funerales*

Estrofas *Salmo 116 (114/115): 1b-2, 3-4a, 5-6, 7-8, 9 & 14, 15-16*

1. *Amo al Señor porque escucha*
   el clamor de mi plegaria;
   Inclinó hacia mí su oído
   el día en que lo llamé.

2. *Me envolvían los lazos de la muerte,*
   estaba preso en las redes fatales,
   me ahogaban la angustia y el pesar,
   pero invoqué el nombre del Señor.

3. *El Señor es muy bueno y justo,*
   nuestro Dios es compasivo;
   El Señor cuida de los pequeños,
   estaba débil y me salvó.

4. *Alma mía, vuelve a tu descanso,*
   que el Señor cuida de ti.
   Ha librado mi alma de la muerte,
   de lágrimas mis ojos y mis pies de dar un paso en falso.

5. *Caminaré en presencia del Señor*
   en la tierra de los vivos.
   cumpliré mis promesas al Señor
   en presencia de todo su pueblo.

6. *Tiene un precio a los ojos del Señor*
   la muerte de sus fieles:
   «¡Mira, Señor, que soy tu servidor, tu servidor y el hijo de tu esclava:
   tú has roto mis cadenas!»

Verses *Ps 116 (114/115): 1b-2, 3-4a, 5-6, 7-8, 9 & 14, 15-16*

1. I love the LORD for he has heard
   the cry of my appeal.
   The LORD was attentive to me
   in the day when I called.

2. They surrounded me, the snares of death,
   with the anguish of the tomb;
   they caught me, sorrow and distress.
   I called on the LORD's name.

3. How gracious is the LORD and just;
   our God has compassion.
   The LORD protects the simple hearts;
   I was helpless so God saved me.

4. Turn back, my soul, to your rest
   for the LORD has been good,
   and has kept my soul from death,
   my eyes from tears, my feet from stumbling.

5. I will walk in the presence of the LORD,
   in the land of the living.
   My vows to the LORD I will fulfill
   before all the people.

6. O precious in the eyes of the LORD
   is the death of the faithful.
   Your servant, LORD, your servant am I;
   you have loosened my bonds.

Saints, Come to Help Him / Her / Them, Holy Ones of God

Funeral Song of Farewell

* Women's voices sing low (alto) C, men's voices sing high (tenor) C

** ***him / her / them***

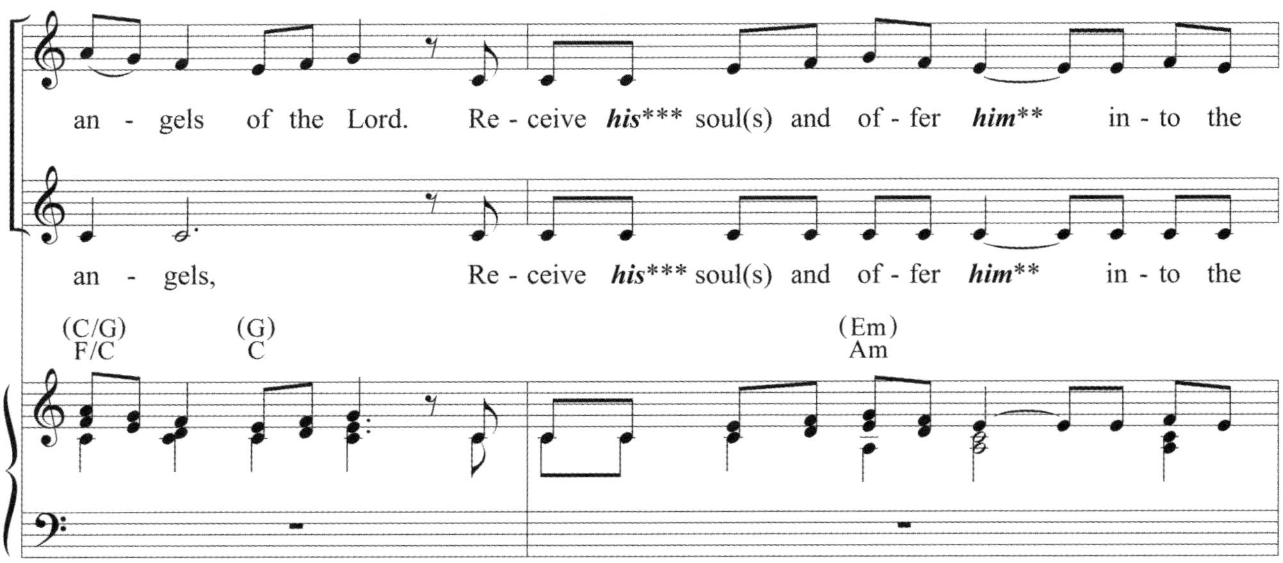

*** ***his / her / their***

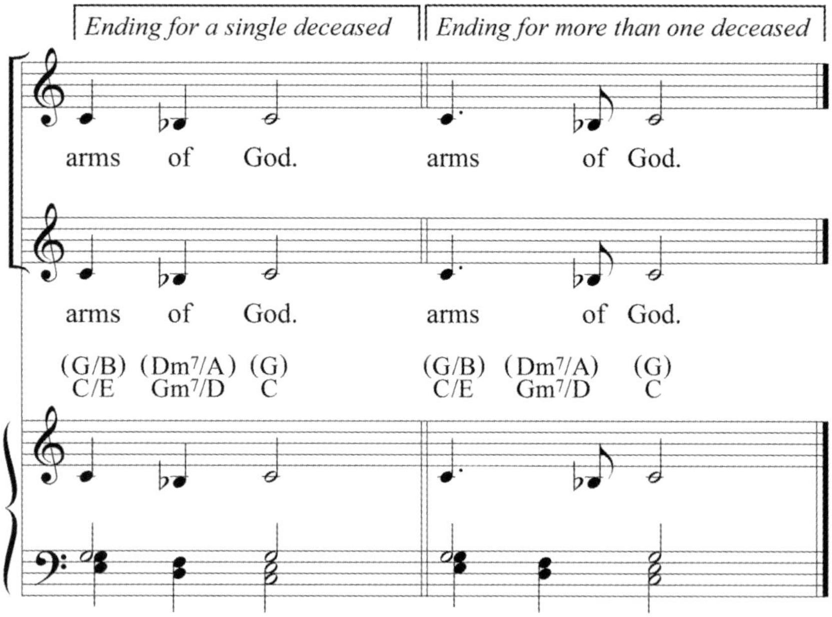

Verses *(Text adapted from the Order of Christian Funerals)*

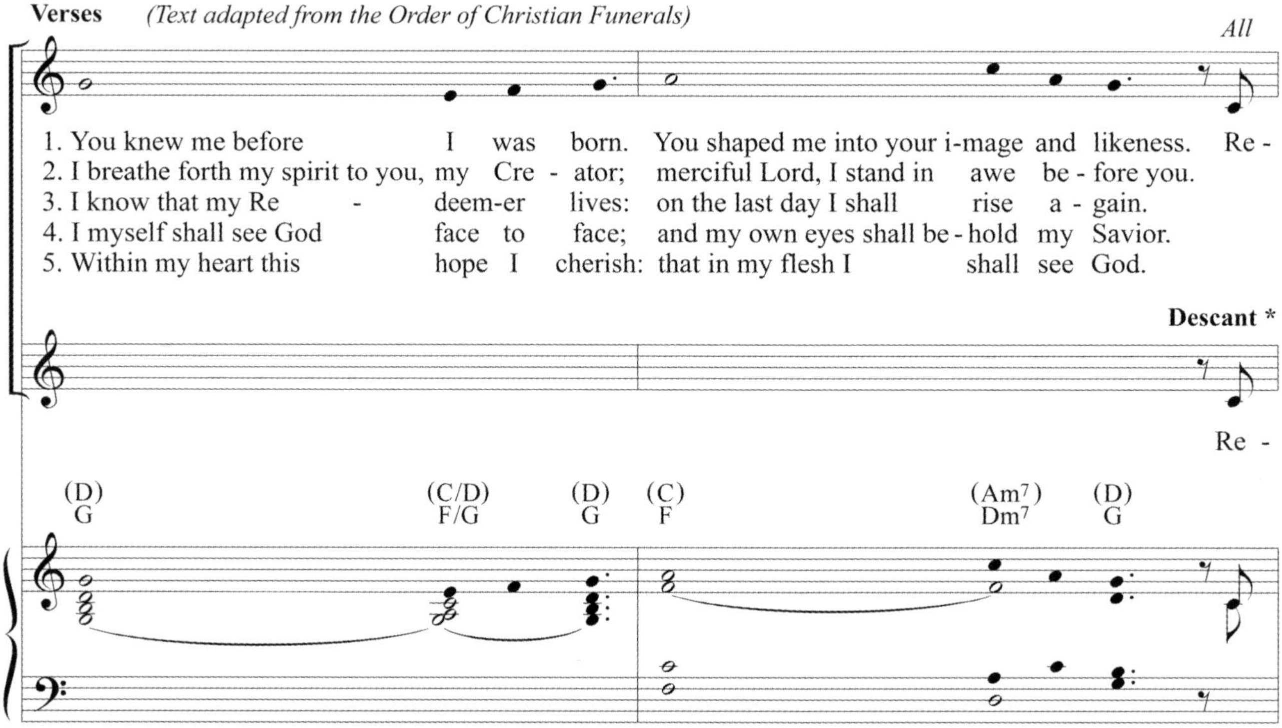

Ending for a single deceased
ceive his*** soul(s) and of - fer him** in - to the arms of God.
ceive his*** soul(s) and of - fer him** in - to the arms of God.
(G) C
(Em) Am
(G/B) C/E
(Dm7/A) Gm7/D
(G) C
Ending for more than one deceased
arms of God.
arms of God.
(G/B) C/E
(Dm7/A) Gm7/D
(G) C

Vengan en Su Ayuda, Santos de Dios

Canción de Despedida para Funerales

* Las voces de las mujeres cantan bajo (alto) C, las voces de los hombres cantan alto (tenor) C

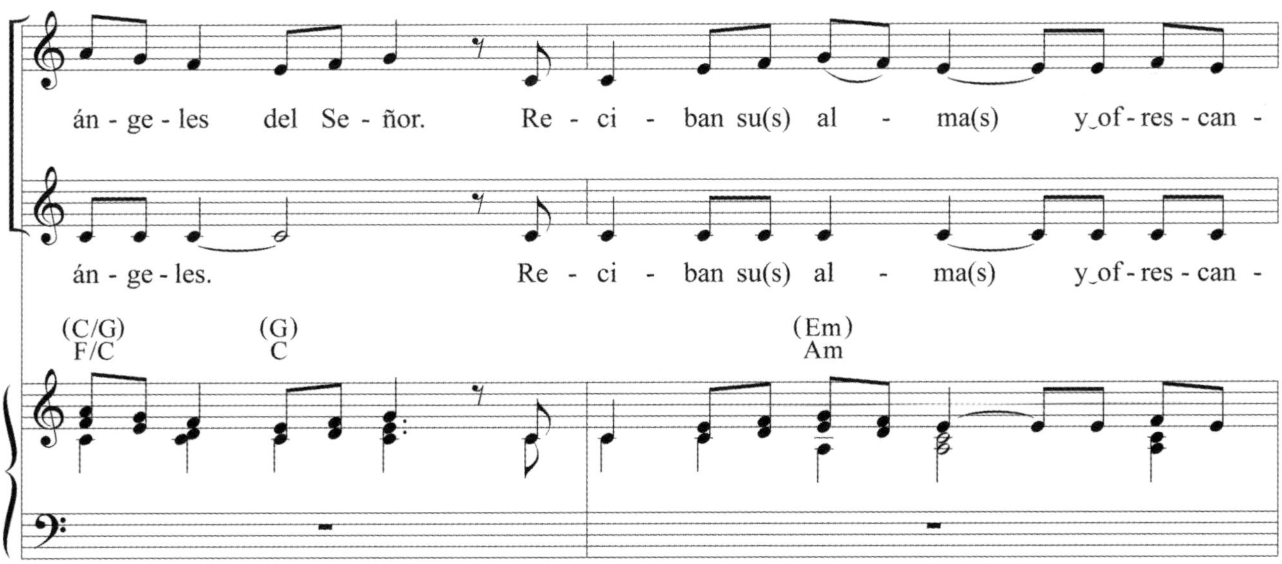

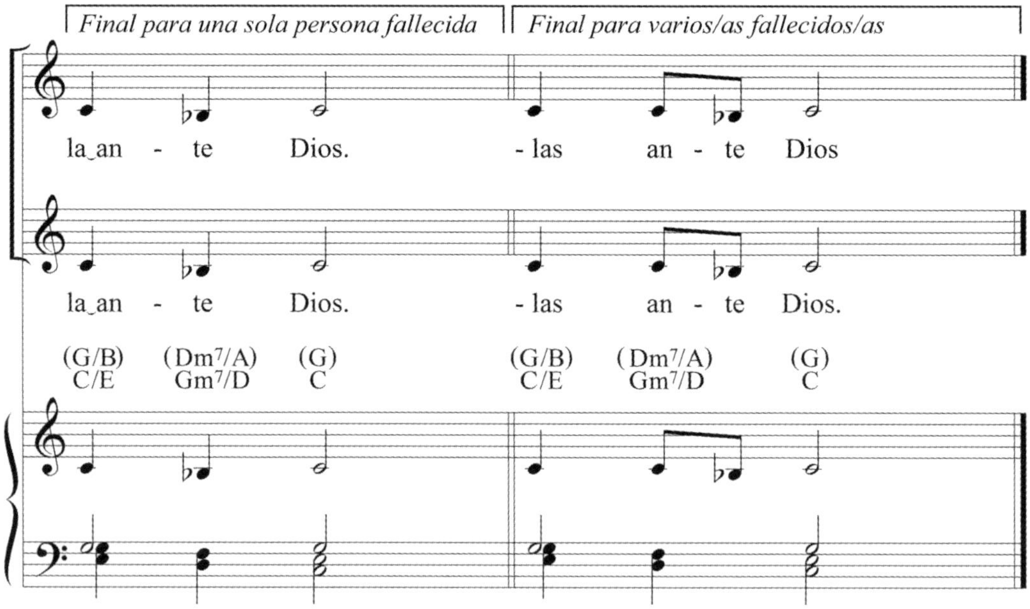

Estrofas *(Texto adaptado del Ritual de Exequias Cristianas)*

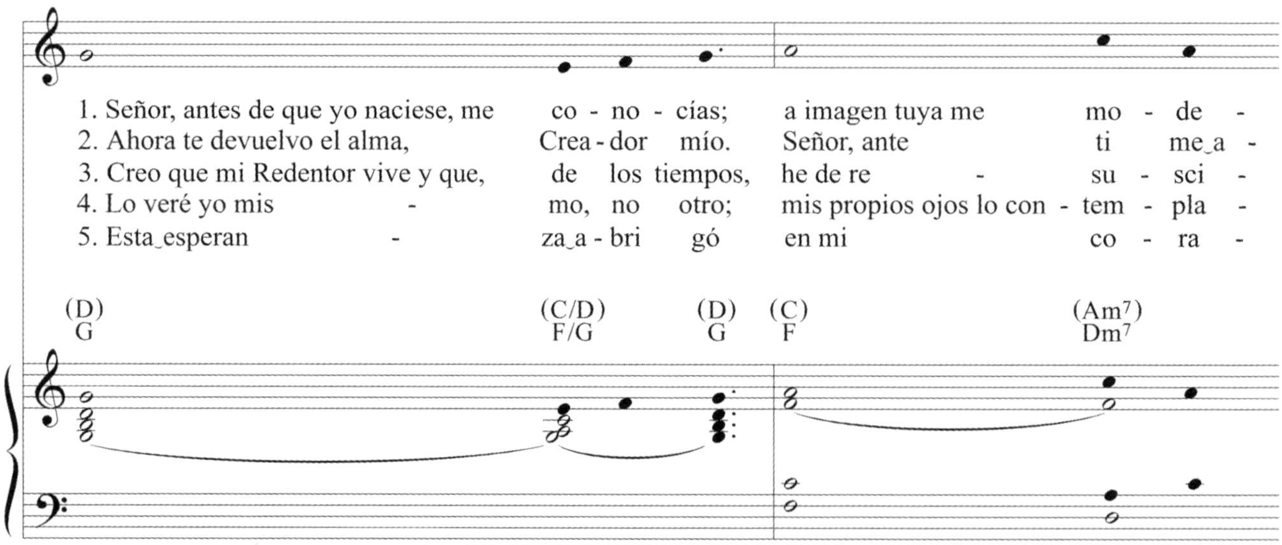

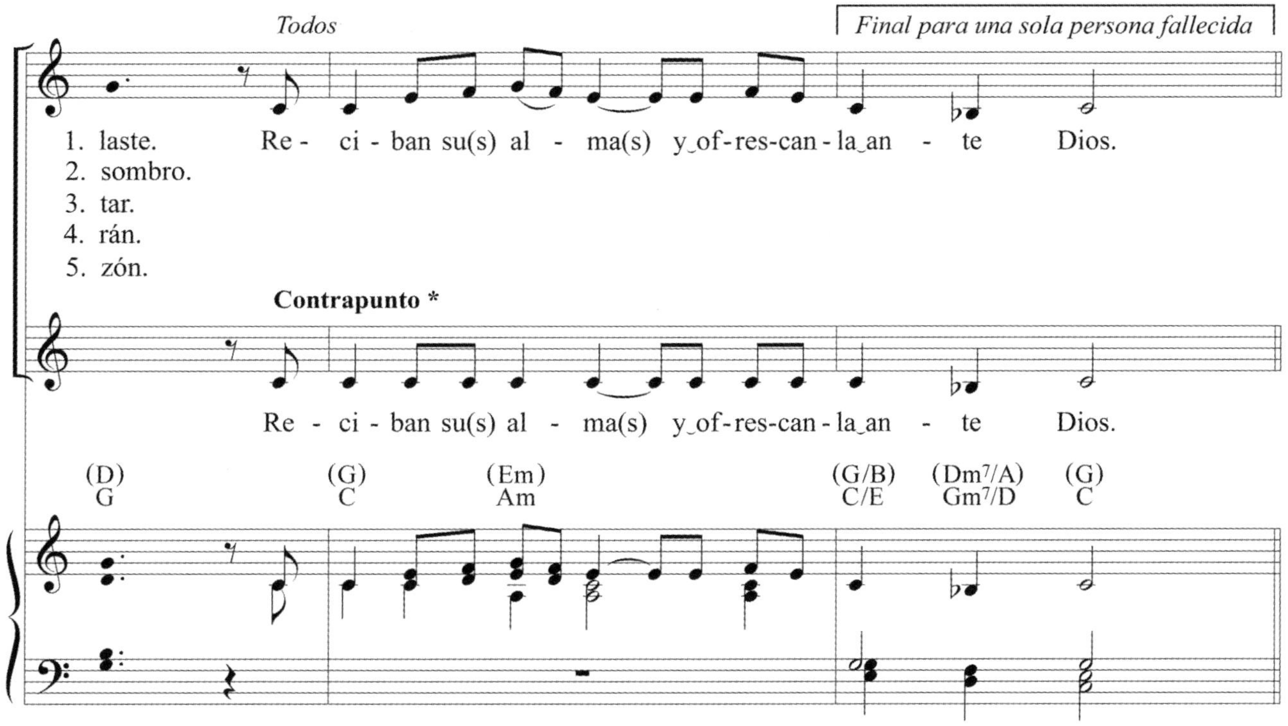
Todos
Final para una sola persona fallecida
1. laste. Re - ci - ban su(s) al - ma(s) y_of-res-can-la_an - te Dios.
2. sombro.
3. tar.
4. rán.
5. zón.
Contrapunto *
Re - ci - ban su(s) al - ma(s) y_of-res-can-la_an - te Dios.
(D) G
(G) C
(Em) Am
(G/B) C/E
(Dm7/A) Gm7/D
(G) C

Final para varios/as fallecidos/as
- las an - te Dios
- las an - te Dios.
(G/B) C/E
(Dm7/A) Gm7/D
(G) C

Apostles' Creed

Presider Introduction (optional)

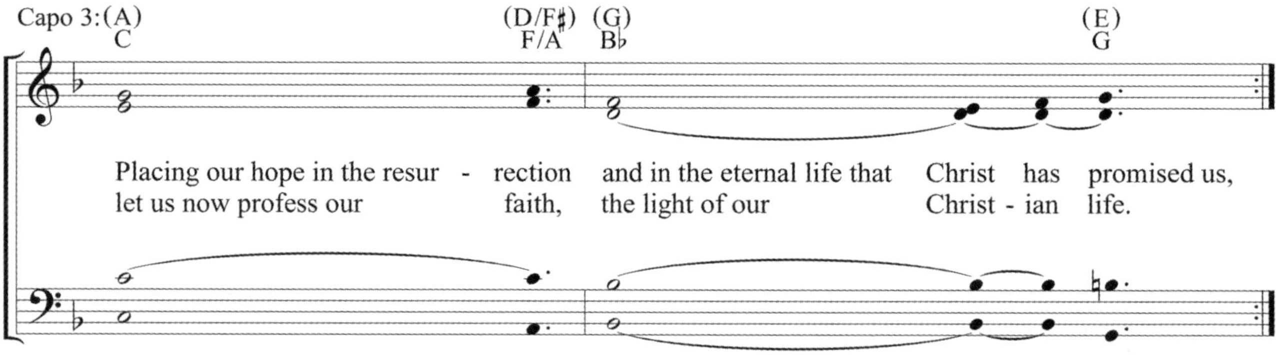

Setting I (melody in the Tenor line)

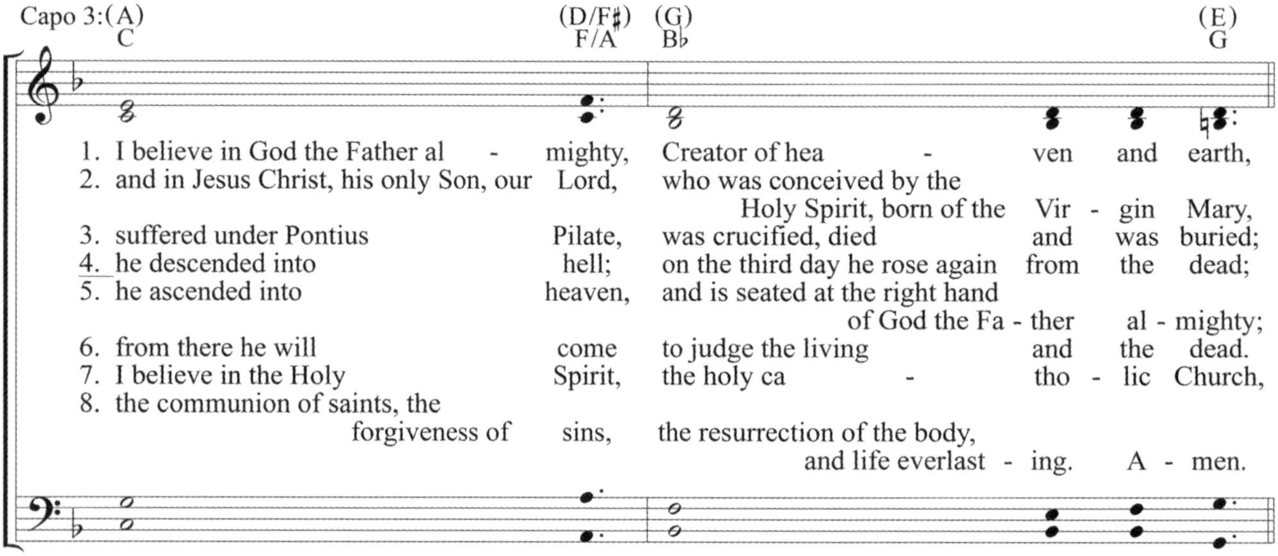

Performance Notes

The chant can be sung as above, with the tenor taking the melody in Setting I, or the soprano in Setting II (SATB). The bass descant remains constant whichever version is used.

The odd-numbered verses could be sung by a solo cantor and the even-numbered verses by choir and all; or everyone can sing all the verses throughout.

Discreet organ accompaniment may be used to sustain the voices. If guitar is used, only one strum per chord symbol should be played.

The Presider's introduction is taken from the Spanish Ritual de Exsequias Cristianas.

Setting II (melody in the Soprano line)

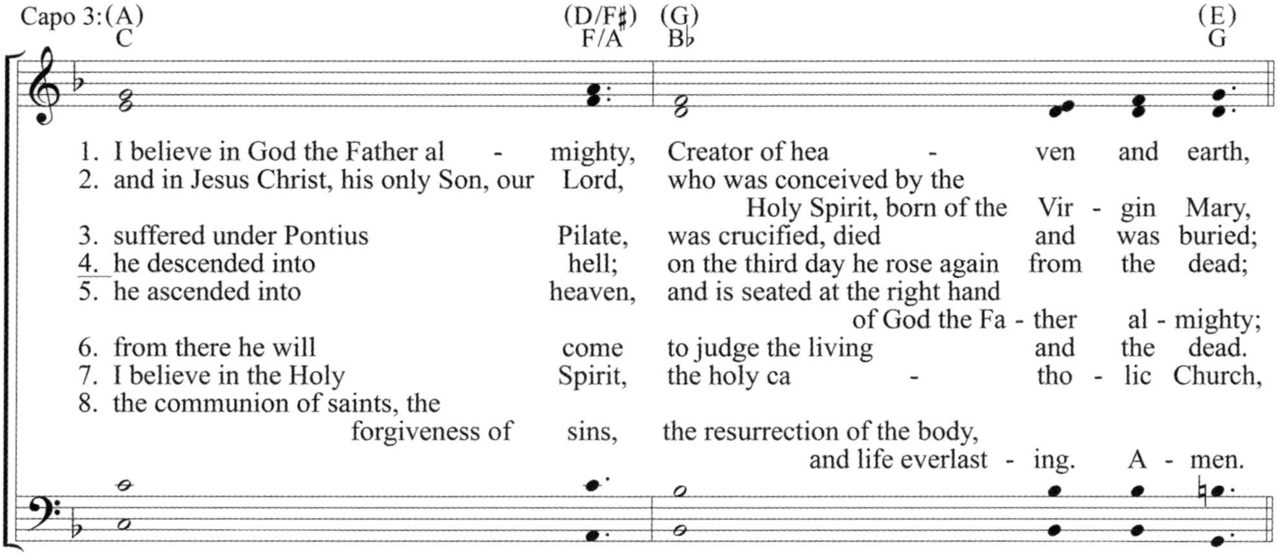

Credo de los Apóstoles

Introducción del Sacerdote (opcional)

Arreglo I (melodía = Tenor)

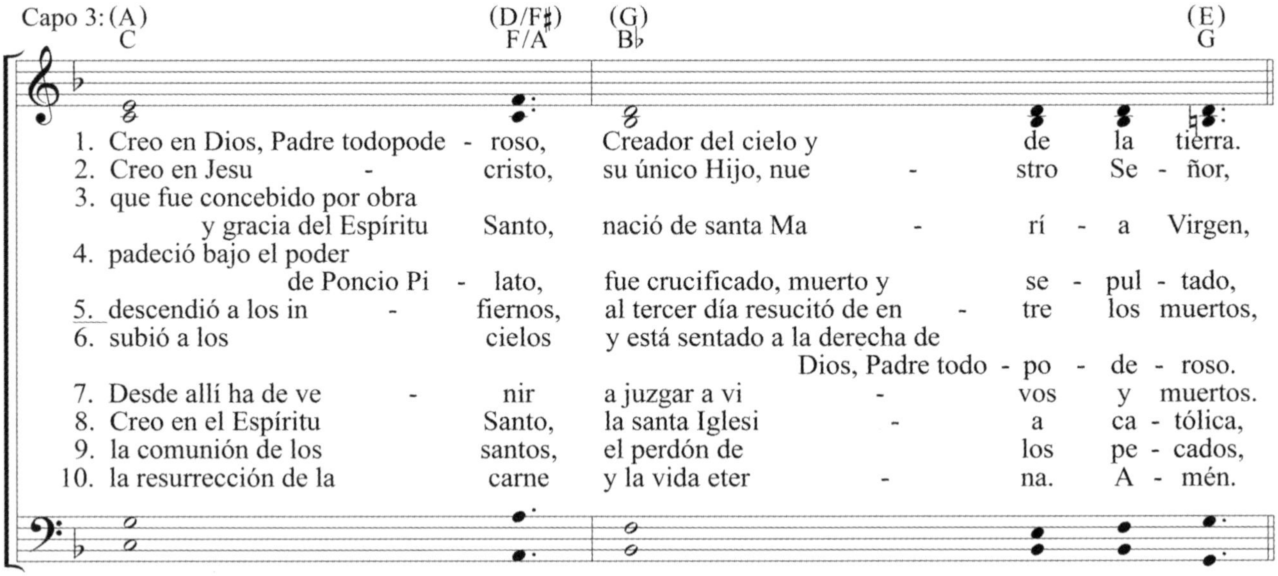

Notas de Interpretación

El canto puede ser cantado igual que el anterior, con el tenor cantando la melodía en arreglo I o la soprano en arreglo II. El contrapunto del bajo se mantiene constante en cualquier versión que se utiliza . Los versos impares podrían ser cantadas por un cantor solista y los versos pares por el coro y toda la asamblea; o todos pueden cantar todos los versos.

Acompañamiento discreto de órgano se puede usar para sostener las voces. Si guitarra se utiliza , sólo un rasgueo por acorde debe ser tocado.

Introducción del Celebrante viene del Ritual de Exequias Cristianas.

Arreglo II (melodía = Soprano)

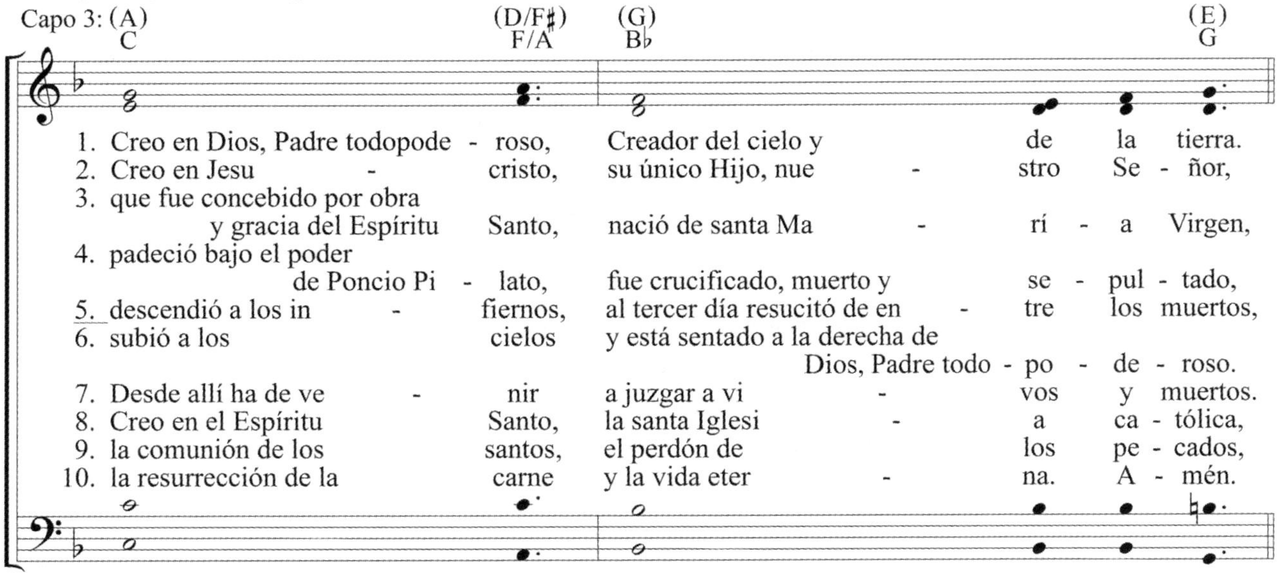

Instrumental Descants

Dichosos Los que Aman — Flute

Antiphon

Thanks Be to God / Gracias a Dios — C Instrument, verses 4-5

Live On in My Love / Vivan en Mi Amor — Flutes

From Clay You Have Shaped Me / De Barro Me Formaste — Oboes

Introduction

After v. 1

After v. 2

After v. 3

Dios Enjugara / God Will Wipe Away — Flutes and Oboes *

* Suggestions are given, but these parts may be played on any suitable combination(s) of C solo instruments.

After v. 2 — Flute (stems up) and Oboe (stems down)

After v. 3 — Oboe I and II

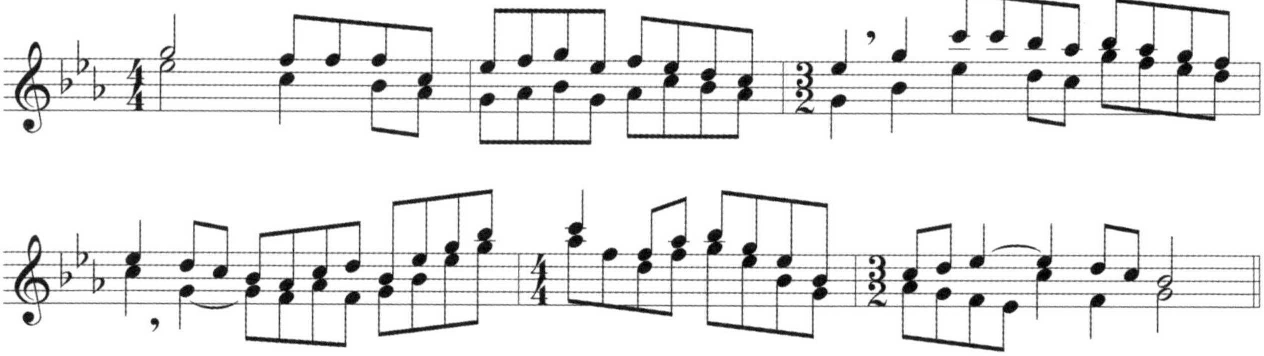

After v. 4 — Flute I and II

Reprint Policy

Before reproducing the assembly graphics on pages 51–59, you must secure the appropriate Reprint License. By using this copyrighted material, you have a moral obligation to the composers whose livelihood depends on receiving a fair compensation for the use of their work. We trust that you value their work and will agree to this requirement. The following Reprint License options are available: 1) the purchase of a $35.00 Annual Reprint License from Liturgical Press (the reporting of titles is not required when reproduced; 2) membership with the licensing service OneLicense.net (you must report the use of titles each time they are reproduced). Each reprint must include the title and the full copyright notice as it appears below the music.

Wedding Responsorial Psalm

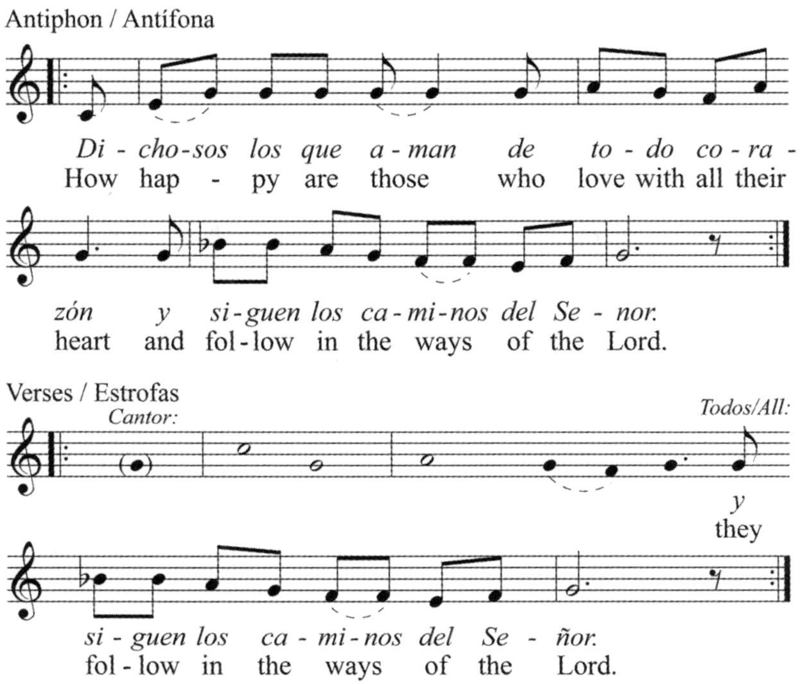

Live On in My Love / *Vivan en Mi Amor*

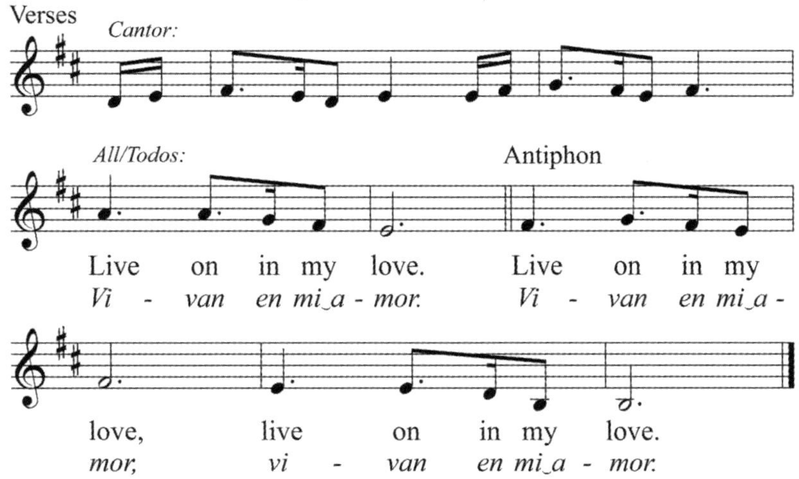

See page 51 for reprint policy.

Wedding Entrance Processional

Antiphon / Antífona

Love Bears All Things / *El Amor Soporta Todo*

Clemente y Bondadoso / Merciful and Tender

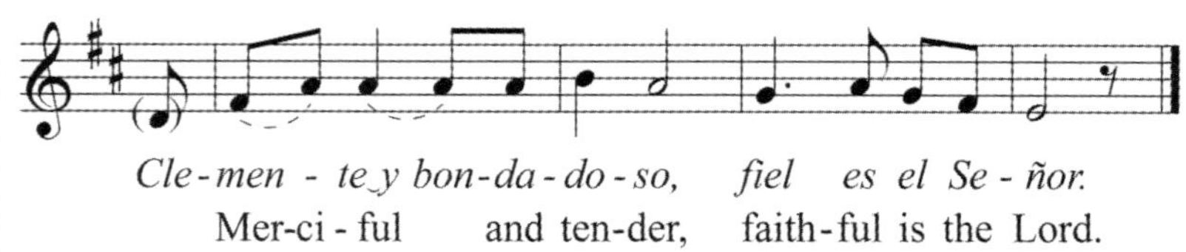

See page 51 for reprint policy.

Thanks be to God! / *¡Gracias a Dios!*

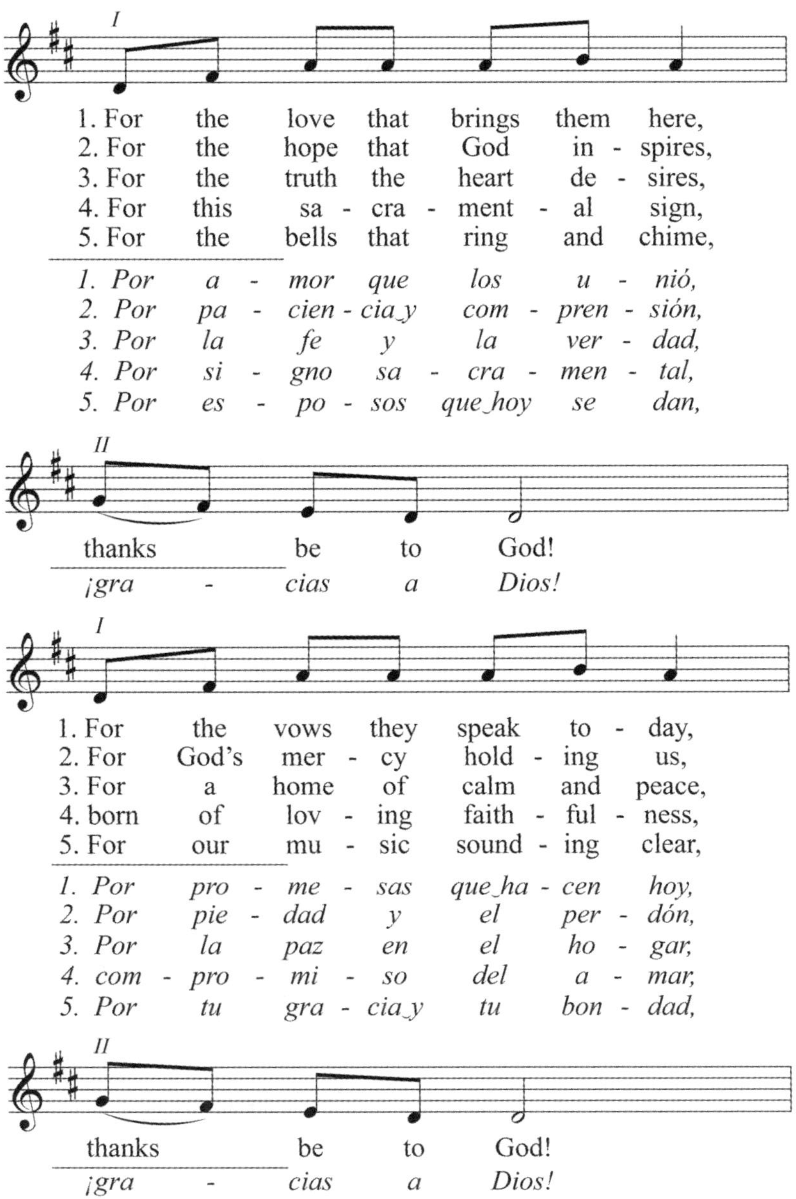

Thanks be to God! / *¡Gracias a Dios!*, cont.

Melody: *Adoro te devote* (Gregorian Chant)
Published and administered by the Liturgical Press, Collegeville, MN 56321.

See page 51 for reprint policy.

Dales el Descanso / Grant Eternal Rest

Antiphon / Antífona

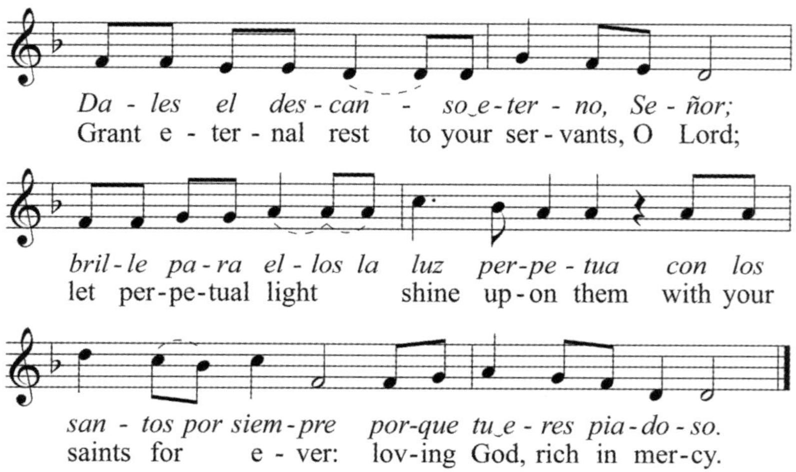

From Clay You Have Shaped Me / *De Barro Me Formaste*

Antiphon / Antífona

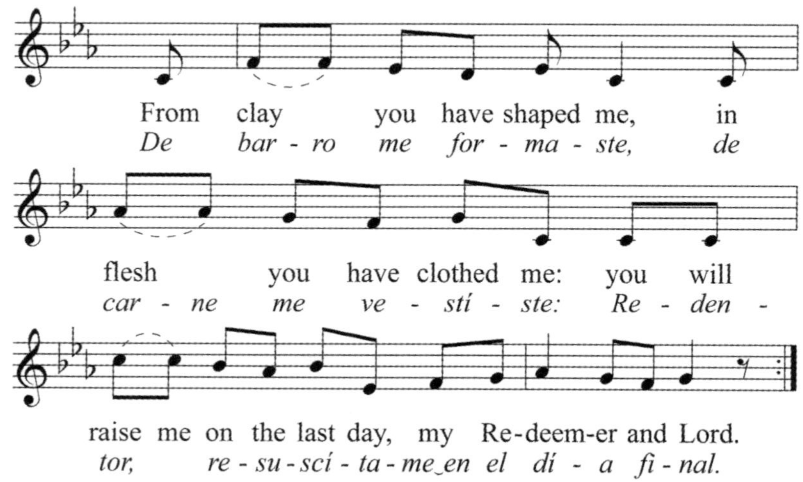

Sing in both languages each time, one after the other, and hum under the verses.
Cantar en ambos idiomas cada vez, una tras otra,
y canturrear con la boca cerrada durante las estrofas.

See page 51 for reprint policy.

Dios Enjugará / God Will Wipe Away

Antífona / Antiphon

Dios Enjugará / God Will Wipe Away, cont.

Estrofas

See page 51 for reprint policy.

Funeral Song of Farewell
(Female Deceased)

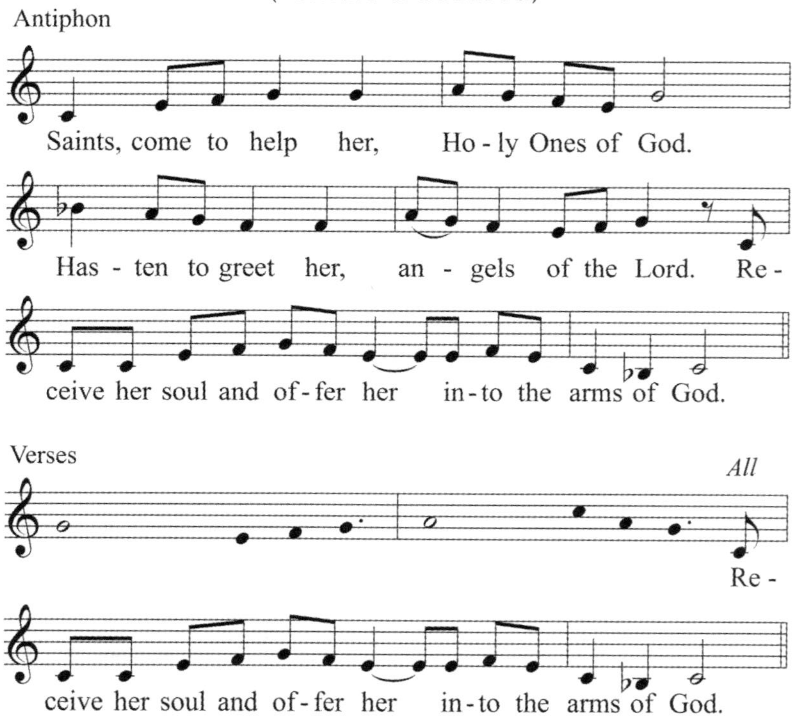

Funeral Song of Farewell
(Male Deceased)

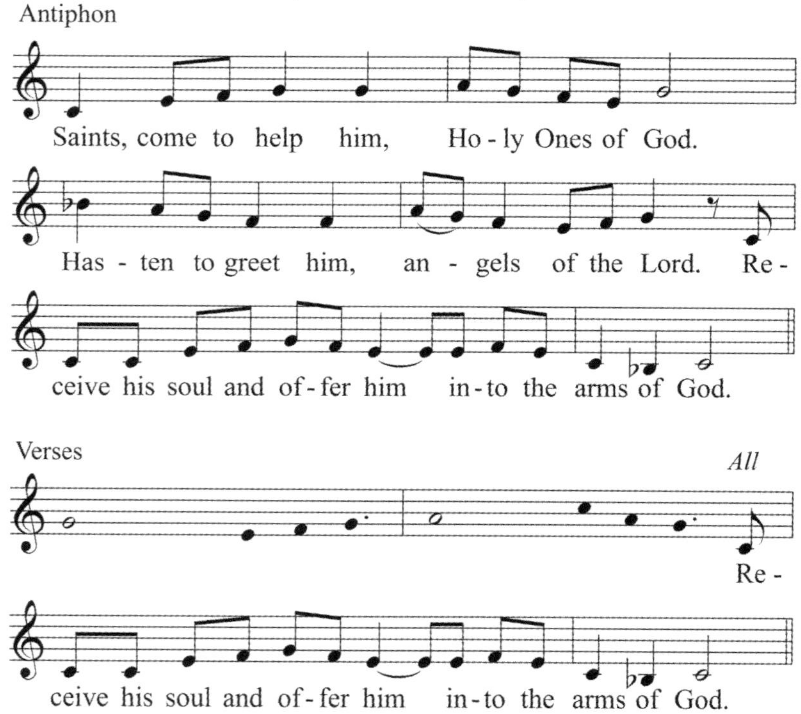

See page 51 for reprint policy.

Funeral Song of Farewell

(Several Deceased)

Antiphon

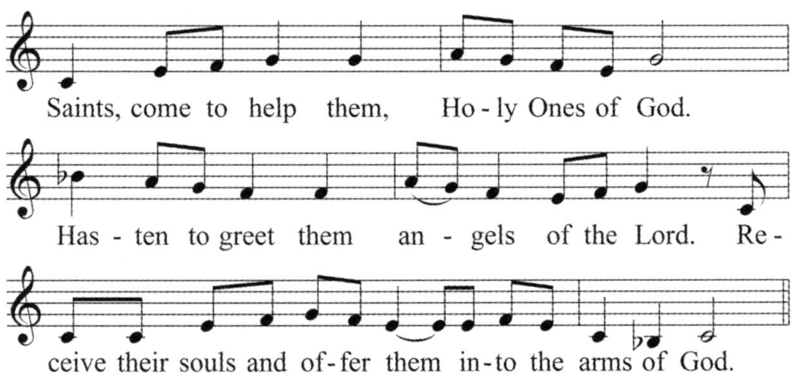

Verses

All

Canción de Despedida para Funerales

(para una sola persona fallecida)

Antífona

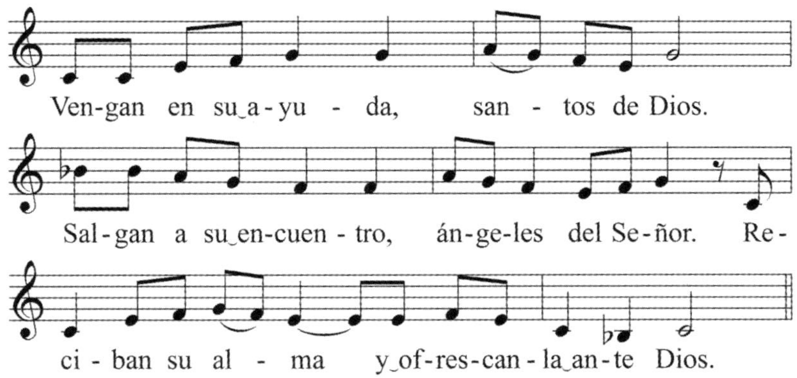

Estrofas

Todos

See page 51 for reprint policy.

Canción de Despedida para Funerales

(para varios/as fallecidos/as)

Antífona

Estrofas

Apostles' Creed (English)

Optional Presider Introduction

Placing our hope in the resurrection
and in the eternal life that Christ has promised us,
let us now profess our faith,
the light of our Christian life.

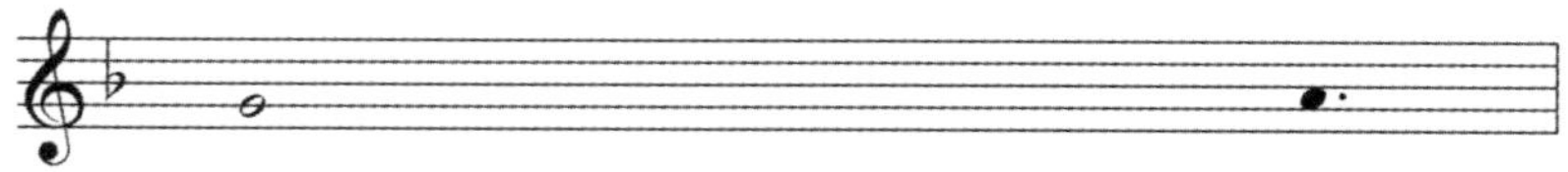

1. I believe in God the Father al - mighty,
2. and in Jesus Christ, his only Son, our Lord,
3. suffered under Pontius Pilate,
4. he descended into hell;
5. he ascended into heaven,
6. from there he will come
7. I believe in the Holy Spirit,
8. the communion of saints, the forgiveness of sins,

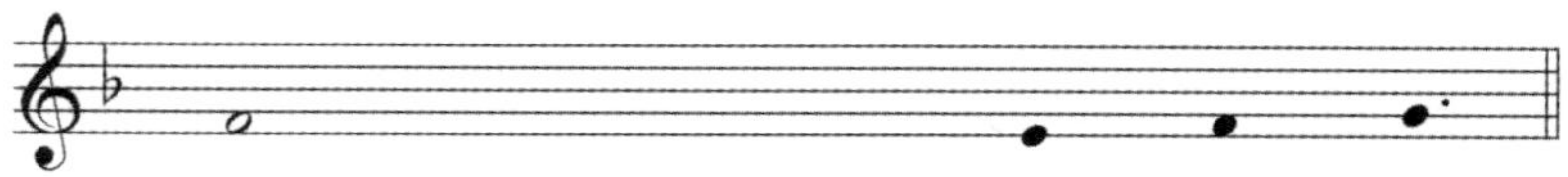

1. Creator of hea - ven and earth,
2. who was conceived by the Holy Spirit, born of the Vir - gin Mary,
3. was crucified, died and was buried;
4. on the third day he rose again from the dead;
5. and is seated at the right hand of God the Fa - ther al - mighty;
6. to judge the living and the dead.
7. the holy ca - tho - lic Church,
8. the resurrection of the body, and life everlast - ing. A - men.

See page 51 for reprint policy.

Credo de los Apóstoles

Introducción del sacerdote (opcional)
Con la esperanza puesta en la resurreción
y en la vida eterna que Cristo nos ha prometido,
profesemos ahora nuestra fe,
luz de nuestra vida cristiana.

1. Creo en Dios, Padre todopode - roso,
2. Creo en Jesu - cristo,
3. que fue concebido por obra - y gracia del Espíritu Santo,
4. padeció bajo el de poder - de Poncio Pi - lato,
5. descendió a los in - fiernos,
6. subió a los cielos
7. Desde allí ha de ve - nir
8. Creo en el Espíritu Santo,
9. la comunión de los santos,
10. la resurrección de la carne

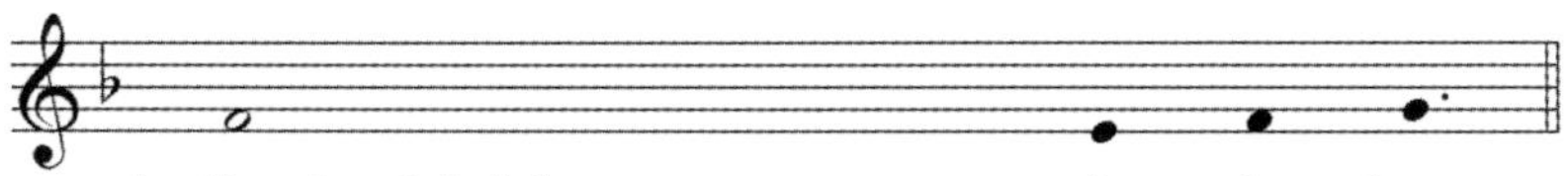

1. Creador del cielo y de la tierra.
2. su único Hijo, nue - stro Se - ñor,
3. nació de santa Ma - rí - a Virgen,
4. fue crucificado, muerto y se - pul - tado,
5. al tercer día resucitó de en - tre los muertos,
6. y está sentado a la derecha de Dios, Padre todo - po - de - roso.
7. a juzgar a vi - vos y muertos.
8. la santa Iglesi - a ca - tólica,
9. el perdón de los pe - cados,
10. y la vida eter - na. A - mén.